Appliqué
Rose Garden

Faye Labanaris

Vintage Album Patterns

American Quilter's Society

P. O. Box 3290 • Paducah, KY 42002-3290

www.AmericanQuilter.com

Located in Paducah, Kentucky, the American Quilter's Society (AQS) is dedicated to promoting the accomplishments of today's quilters. Through its publications and events, AQS strives to honor today's quiltmakers and their work and to inspire future creativity and innovation in quiltmaking.

EDITOR: BARBARA SMITH
GRAPHIC DESIGN: ELAINE WILSON
COVER DESIGN: MICHAEL BUCKINGHAM
PHOTOGRAPHY: CHARLES R. LYNCH

Library of Congress Cataloging-in-Publication Data

Labanaris, Faye
    Appliqué rose garden : vintage album patterns / by Faye Labanaris.
        p.cm.
    Summary: "Showcase of 48 rose patterns from 1800s and early 1900s including wreaths, cross sprays, stemmed roses, paper-cut designs, and floral arrangements. Author shows techniques for adding texture to rose stems, leaves, buds, and blossoms including making bias stems, stuffed roses, and embroidered flower and leaf details"--Provided by publisher.
    Includes bibliographical references.
    ISBN 1-57432-884-0
    1. Appliqué--Patterns. 2. Quilting. 3. Album quilts. 4. Rose in art. I. Title.

    TT779.L23 2005
    746.44'5041--dc22

            2005006931CIP

Additional copies of this book may be ordered from the American Quilter's Society, PO Box 3290, Paducah, KY 42002-3290; 800-626-5420 (orders only please); or online at www.AmericanQuilter.com. For all other inquiries, call 270-898-7903.

Copyright © 2005, Faye Labanaris

All rights reserved. No part of this book may be reproduced, stored in any retrieval system, or transmitted in any form, or by any means including but not limited to electronic, mechanical, photocopy, recording, or otherwise, without the written consent of the author and publisher. Patterns may be copied for personal use only.

Dedication

This book is dedicated to

Elly Sienkiewicz

with
affection, admiration and gratitude.

Her passion, dedication, and love
of
Baltimore Album Quilts
have inspired me to create
this volume of vintage rose album patterns.

Thank you, Elly!

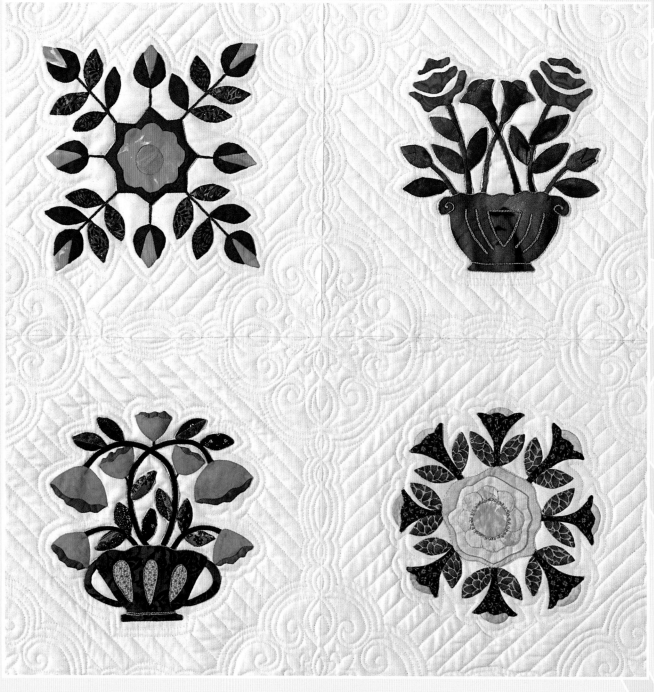

FANCY ROSES (detail) made by the author, quilted by Ellen Peters, Laconia, New Hampshire

Contents

Introduction

My inspiration for this book came while I was working on my *Garden View Applique* book. There were so many wonderful vintage floral patterns in it, that I thought how wonderful it would be to make a quilt with just rose album patterns. Little did I realize that, a few years later, I would be submitting a proposal for an entire book of vintage rose patterns … on Valentine's Day. I completed the four quilts and submitted this manuscript to my publisher, American Quilter's Society, on Valentine's Day the following year.

Our quiltmaking ancestors were talented and creative. Their legacy of quilts and designs survives today and continues to inspire us to build on the past with our present-day resources. Whenever a special block or quilt was to be made for a wedding, the rose was the chosen flower, stitched to symbolize love. The rose is a beautiful flower that has been associated from time immemorial with love and beauty. Roses were lovingly carried as cuttings when the pioneers left their homes and ventured out into the wilderness to settle new areas of the country. They brought few family treasures with them because space was at a premium, but they always found room for a few stems of a rosebush, from their families' gardens, to grow in their new surroundings. These old roses, such as Harrison's Yellow, have been found growing all along the Oregon Trail and at sites of old homesteads and in old cemeteries. Their hardiness has enabled them to survive.

Appliquéd quilts tended to be used for special occasions, whereas pieced quilts served as more utilitarian covers for warmth. Because appliqué is not as precise or geometric as piecing, there was a tendency for quilters to depart from the pattern to create their own artistic interpretations of a design. Each maker stitched her own personality into a quilt or album block, resulting in many variations of similar designs. The names of the blocks were also changed, along with their appearance, depending on the maker's whim. Album quilts, which are composed of many different theme-related blocks, were made for special occasions, such as wedding and friendship quilts, because many different people could contribute blocks.

This book is filled with a love of roses and quilts. The beauty and ageless appeal of rose designs from 150 years ago are captured in this volume for you to create your own rose garden of quilts. Each quiltmaker, past or present, stitches her own personality into each rose block. That personality or personal touch adds to and enhances the beauty of the album legacy. The threads of the past so lovingly stitched are preserved and enhanced for future generations to enjoy. Together, the combination results in a lovely collection of rose blocks for album quilts I hope you will enjoy making.

And I will make thee beds of roses
And a thousand fragrant posies.

Christopher Marlow, 1564–1593
"The Passionate Shepherd to His Love"

Getting Started

I have often tried to grow lovely roses in my garden, but the harsh New England winters and a very shady garden have resulted in many failures. Only the old-fashioned roses that were on the property when we bought our home more than 30 years ago have survived and thrived. However, roses stitched on fabric are another story. That I can do! I enjoyed working on these four rose album quilts, and while I may not have many beautiful roses in my garden, I can have beautiful roses on my quilts to enjoy. I hope you will enjoy putting together your own rose garden from these vintage album patterns.

Creating a rose quilt is a lot of fun. You can choose the album style and have each block made from a different pattern, or go with a more formal or symmetrical look. Whichever style you choose to make, be it a bed-sized quilt with 48 blocks, a four-block wallhanging, or a single-rose-block pillow, happiness is in the journey of selecting lovely fabrics, stitching beautiful flowers, and adding delightful embroidered details. For the four quilts that I have put together, each was made with 12 different blocks in this series. Each quilt has a different theme and personality, ranging from informal folk art to a more formal style. They were fun to stitch and a pleasure to look at when completed.

In stitching the various rose blocks, I thought it would be fun to use a variety of textures and techniques for the rose stems, leaves, buds, and blossoms. I have included some of these techniques for you to mix and match and use in place of traditional sewing methods. I have also included a set of patterns for basic buds and blossoms, and you can change these patterns to suit your taste. After all, our ancestors looked at previously sewn appliquéd blocks and made them their own by changing them as they stitched.

Selecting Fabrics

We are so blessed today to have such a lovely variety of fabrics to choose from. Beautiful hand-painted, dyed, marbleized, and batik fabrics lend themselves to beautiful rose petals and leaves. Selecting the combinations is a pleasure that will result in beautiful rose blocks.

BACKGROUND FABRICS

Different background fabrics produce different looks in your finished blocks. For the formal quilt FANCY ROSES, I chose an ivory polished cotton. For FOLK ART ROSES, I used a variety of tan prints in many different shades. In A COUNTRY ROSE GARDEN, I stitched the roses onto hand-dyed, blue-sky fabric and used a variety of greens and a stone-wall print to complete the garden quilt. With RENOIR'S ROSE GARDEN, I fell in love with a medley print collection and used as many of the fabrics as possible to make the blocks.

FANCY ROSES (close-up, see quilt on page 67)

FOLK ART ROSES (close-up, see quilt on page 25)

A COUNTRY ROSE GARDEN (close-up, see quilt on page 39)

RENOIR'S ROSE GARDEN (close-up, see quilt on page 53)

LEAF AND FLOWER FABRICS

You can never have too many green fabrics in your collection (fig. 1, page 10). Go through your fabrics and cut strips or squares from all your greens. Actually, 6"–9" squares are best because you can cut small bias stems from them. These small amounts of fabric can easily be kept within reach in a basket, and you'll have a lot of wonderful shades and prints for your leaf selections. Keep the smaller scraps in a separate see-through plastic bag, which will allow you to reach in and find the right piece without having to empty the bag. Go through your fabric collection and select colors for your roses. Cut squares of about 6"–12". There are so many colors in roses, that almost any flower-colored fabric will work (fig. 2, page 11). Shaded fabrics are wonderful in that you can cut many variations from the same piece of fabric. Keep the original lengths of fabric in a nearby pile so you can access them easily if you need more of a particular piece. This will save you from having to go back into your collection to look for the fabric again. Select fabrics that have actual roses printed on them (fig. 3, pages 10–11). The printed leaves on these fabrics are great to use for some of your leaves.

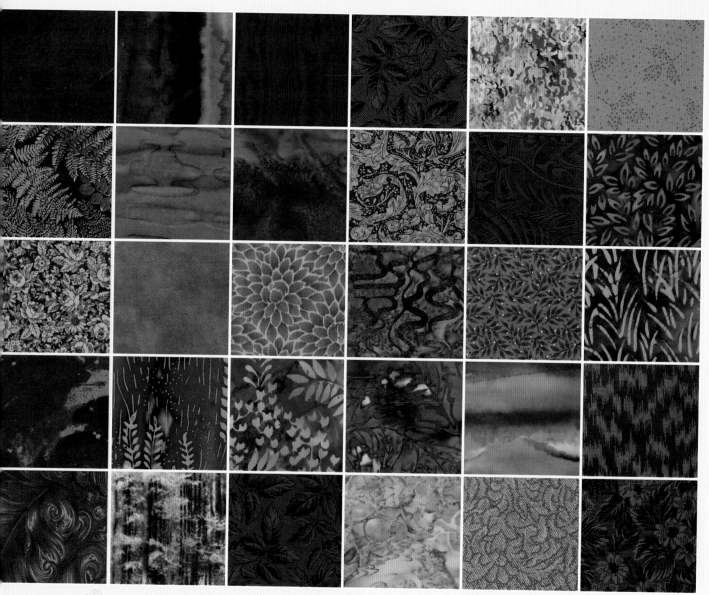

Fig. 1. *Samples of leaf fabrics*

Fig. 3. *Samples of prints for wholecloth roses*

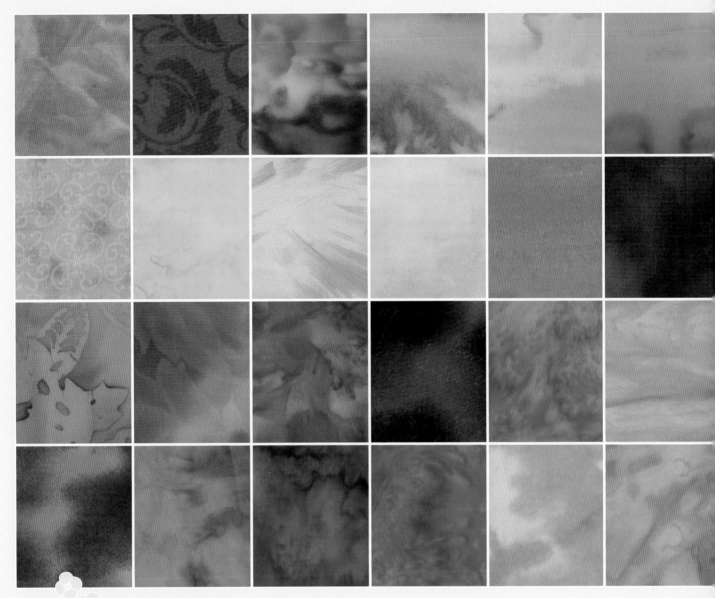

Fig. 2. *Samples of flower fabrics*

Making Stems

A number of bias-stem techniques are presented here, but stems can be made from other materials, too, such as yarns and trims.

TRADITIONAL BIAS STEMS

❋ This method involves cutting a strip of fabric, anywhere from ¾" to 1" wide, on the bias.

❋ Fold the strip in half right side out.

❋ Place the strip on the background, aligning the raw edges with the outer curve of the stem-line tracing (fig. 4).

❋ Using a small running stitch, sew the stem to the background, about one-fourth to one-third of the way in from the raw edges.

❋ Fold the strip over the line of stitching, covering the raw edges, and sew along the folded edge of the stem.

Fig. 4. *Traditional bias stems: (a) place raw edges on outer curve, (b) sew outer curve, (c) fold strip over the stitching, and (d) sew along the fold.*

FOLDED BIAS STEMS

A bias strip of fabric can also be folded into thirds and basted down the middle on the machine for a result similar to the bias-bar method (fig. 5). This method works great if you need a small number of prepared bias stems. The strips can also be used for basket weaving. If the weavers are straight, then the strips can be cut on the straight of grain to save fabric.

BIAS-BAR STEMS

These long, thin flexible bars, made of metal or nylon, are used for sewing bias tubes. Follow the directions on the bias-bar packaging for stitching a variety of sizes of stems.

FUSED BIAS STEMS

Fused bias is a product you can buy on a roll. Place the strip on the drawn stem line and iron the fused fabric into place. Stitch it down afterward for permanent placement. The disadvantage to this method is that you are limited in the shades of green that you can find.

SKINNY STEMS

For really skinny stems (⅛" wide), you can fold fused bias stems in half, with the fused sides together, and iron them in place. These can be couched to make the tiny stems that connect to the main stem.

STEMS FROM TRIMS

There are so many wonderful trims and cordings on the market. Once you start using trims in your appliqué work, you'll seek out many sources for your collection (fig. 6). The advantage to this technique is that you can use a narrow width for tiny stems or a textured trim for hairy stems. The texture of trims adds interest to a block and makes sewing stems fast, fun, and easy.

Fig. 5. *Strip folded in thirds and basted*

Fig. 6. *Trim used for stems: (a) couched cording, (b) couched trim, (c) stitched trim*

* Use a wooden toothpick to draw a tiny bead of white glue along the stem line.

* Place the trim on top of the glue and press it into position.

* After the glue dries, stitch the trim down with a few tacking stitches from behind, or use decorative or matching thread to couch the trim.

YARN STEMS

There are many beautiful yarns available today. If they are too thin, just twist several lengths together and couch the resulting cord in position, again using a glue line as a holding medium. If you try to stitch the yarn without the glue, the stem will tend to wander a bit and not lie straight.

Fig. 7. *Reverse appliquéd split leaf*

Making Leaves

Feel free to use your imagination when making leaves. It's perfectly fine to substitute leaves from a different pattern, or you can reduce or enlarge leaf patterns to change the look of a design. Here are some ideas for making leaves:

FUSED LEAVES

Leaves can be positioned with a fusible then stitched down. A decorative stitch can be added to the cut edge to enhance the leaf.

SPLIT LEAF

This technique adds color and a touch of realism to your leaves, and it's great for using up small bits of fabric.

* Stitch two different fabric pieces together (use pieces about 1¼" x 3"–6").

* Center a see-through leaf template on the seam line and trace the leaf shape with a fabric marking pencil or pen.

* Cut the fabric leaf ¼" outside the drawn line. Iron the center seam allowance open rather than to one side.

* At the points, trim away the seam allowance at an angle to eliminate bulk.

REVERSE APPLIQUÉD SPLIT LEAF

If the leaf points would still be too bulky when the edges are turned, use the split leaf as a reverse appliqué.

* Cut out a leaf shape from the background fabric, allowing a generous turn-under allowance.

* Position the split leaf fabric underneath the background, turn under the allowance, and appliqué in place (fig. 7).

Making Roses

There are a number of ways of making roses. You can cut an entire blossom from a rose print to make a wholecloth rose; cut a flat rose, such as one of the sugar cookie flower patterns shown on page 18; or try your hand at various dimensional techniques. Several ideas are presented here:

GRADATED PETALS

This method has the advantage that you are sewing a small unit to a larger piece of fabric, which is much easier than sewing two small units together. The method works equally well by hand or machine. For an example of a rose with gradated petals, refer to the Whig Rose block (Fig. 8). Gradated rose petals that range from dark to light can be easily accomplished, as follows:

❋ Make a freezer-paper tracing of your chosen rose pattern with its individual petals.

❋ Cut the template for the first petal, the outermost one.

❋ Mark the template shape on the fabric and cut the fabric piece with a scant ¼" turn-under allowance.

❋ Sew the petal to a larger piece of fabric that you've selected for the second petal.

❋ Position the template for the second petal next to the first one.

❋ Mark and cut the second petal as before. Then appliqué both petals to the fabric you've selected for the third petal.

❋ Continue in this manner until all the petals have been sewn together.

Fig. 8. *FOLK ART ROSES, Whig Rose block, page 31*

Of all flowers,
Methinks a rose is best.

John Fletcher and William Shakespeare
"The Two Noble Kinsmen"

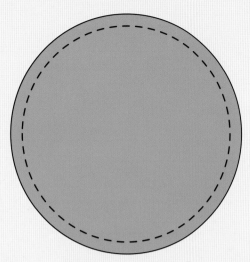

Fig. 9. *Stitch around the outside of the circle.*

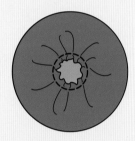

Fig. 10. *Gather the stitches.*

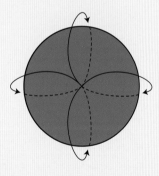

Fig. 11. *Use four stitches to gather into petals.*

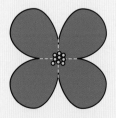

Fig. 12. *Embellish the flower center.*

FOUR-PETAL DIMENSIONAL POSIES

You will see a number of these small flowers in several of the blocks.

❋ Cut a 2½" to 4" circle.

❋ Sew a row of basting stitches all around the outside edge of the circle (fig. 9).

❋ Gather the stitches tightly (fig. 10)

❋ Flatten the piece to form a flat yo-yo.

❋ Using several strands of matching thread, come up through the center of the flower and go over the outer edge and back into the center again, pulling the thread tight to form a petal division.

❋ Repeat this stitch three more times to make four petals (fig. 11).

❋ When the last petal is secured in the center, add gold floss French knots or beads before adding the posy to your block (fig. 12).

MAKING STUFFED ROSES

Roses can be stitched in traditional appliqué, or the individual petals can be stuffed for a more three-dimensional appearance (fig. 13, page 17).

You can stuff a petal or a wholecloth rose with a thin layer of batting as you appliqué it in place.

❋ Cut one to three layers of a soft, thin batting in the shape of the petal or whole flower. Each batting piece should be cut ¼"–⅛" smaller than the previous layer. You are creating a tiered effect.

❋ Stack the batting pieces like a wedding cake then turn the stack upside down.

❋ Glue-baste only the smallest layer to the background fabric.

✳ Cut the appliqué piece with a ½" allowance to make it easier to turn the edges over the padded layers. Then appliqué the piece over the batting onto the background fabric.

Sometimes after appliquéing a rose, you may decide that it looks too flat. You can remove all the stitches and start over with a padded layer. However, there's an easier method:

✳ Turn the block over and make a small slit in the background fabric in the middle of the stitched rose.

✳ Gently slide in some batting and poke it around with a chopstick. My preference is wool batting because you can pull off a few layers of fibers, if needed. Polyester batting also works nicely. Silk batting is a wonderful luxury that adds a really soft look. Be sure to push the batting to the outer edges of the petals.

✳ Stitch up the back slit, taking care to make the edges just meet and not overlap.

Making Rosebuds

ROSEBUD CASE

To make an easy calyx (outer case) for a rosebud, cut it from Ultrasuede®. This product needs no needle-turn appliqué. The exact and intricate shape can be cut quite easily with small, sharp scissors.

✳ Use a fine-point permanent pen to trace the bud case template on the wrong side of the Ultrasuede, which is the darker and smoother side. Mark this side with a small *x*.

✳ Cut the piece just inside the drawn line. Position the bud case on the background and use a glue stick to hold it in place.

✳ Select a neutral fine thread. Taupe-colored silk thread is wonderful and almost invisible.

Fig. 13. *Stuffed roses with embroidered accents*

Fig. 14. *Bud case with outline embroidery*

Rose Variations

Wherever roses are shown in the patterns, you can substitute a different type of rose, if you like. Here are some possibilities.

Use a sharp milliner's (straw) needle, such as a size 10 or 11, and just catch the side edge of the bud case to the background fabric. The closer your stitches are, the more the piece will curve toward the background fabric.

✳ If you want to enhance the dimensional effect, you can embroider an outline stitch around the bud case in the same or a slightly contrasting color (Fig. 14, page 17). Just before taking the last few stitches, you can add a tiny bit of batting for a padded effect, if you like.

DIMENSIONAL ROSEBUDS

Folded fabric can be used for making dimensional rosebuds to insert in the bud cases. Referring to figure 15, fold a 2"–3" circle in half. Then fold the half circle in thirds. Stitch across the bottom and gather the stitches. The gathering step can be omitted if you want a flat folded rosebud. In that case, you may have to trim the bottom side edges slightly, tapering it to fit into the bud case.

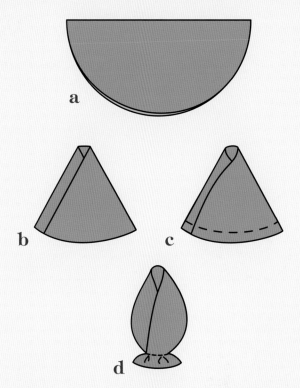

Fig. 15. *Folded rose buds: (a) fold the circle in half, (b), fold the half circle in thirds, (c) stitch across the bottom, (d) gather the stitches.*

Rosebud Variations

In nature, rosebuds come in an amazing variety of shapes and sizes. Here are a few to add to your blocks.

Fig. 16. *Rose with embroidered stamens*

Embroidered Details

All roses have lovely centers with stamens. Capturing this natural look on your appliquéd roses will definitely add a finishing touch. To embroider the stamens, sew radiating lines of straight stitches, in varying lengths, by using a variety of golden shades of yellow thread and topping each stamen with a French knot. The result will be a lovely realistic center (fig. 16).

FRENCH KNOTS

The variation in knots comes in the number of times you twist the thread onto the needle and the number of threads used. Usually, I twist the thread one, two, or three times. If you want bigger knots, twist more thread on the needle or use several strands of thread. A variety of thread colors can be used in combination for a shaded knot.

MULTIPLE FALSE FRENCH KNOTS

Take a 12" length of embroidery floss with all the strands, or make a mixture of individual thread colors. Tie a knot in the middle of the floss and continue looping and tying loosely pulled knots down the length of the floss. Leave about ¼"–½" between each knot. Use a needle and doubled thread to anchor each knot to the rose center. Meander the connecting threads or stitch the knots close together and clip the connecting threads for a fringed look (fig. 17). You can fill in with an assortment of beads for a sparkling dewy effect.

MORE DETAILS

Additional embroidery can be used to enhance the individual petals as well as adding veins to leaves, thorns to the stems, and rose hairs to rosebuds. Use fancy machine embroidery stitches for stems, veins, and petals. Fabric pens can also be used for ink work on leaf veins,

Fig. 17. *Flower centers with false French knots*

Embroidery Stitches

Adding hand or machine embroidered details will enhance your rose block with touches of realism.

Embroidery Stitches
right-handed

stem (outline) stitch

buttonhole stitch

chain stitch

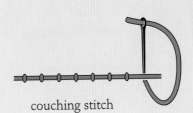

split stitch

French knot

couching stitch

Embroidery Stitches
left-handed

stem (outline) stitch

buttonhole stitch

chain stitch

split stitch

French knot

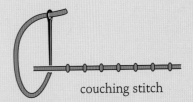

couching stitch

rose hairs, and thorns. Once you get started adding details, you won't be able to stop. Looking at real roses as well as lovely roses drawn in gardening books will spur your creativity. Just enjoy!

Woven Baskets

Gather flowers, buds, and leaves from several block patterns to make a charming flower arrangement in a woven basket (see the Basket of Roses and Berries block in figure 18). Here are the steps for making a woven basket:

⁎ For the basket weavers, cut ¾"–1" wide straight-grain strips of fabric.

⁎ Fold the strips into thirds along their length and baste.

⁎ Iron the strips flat then arrange them on a background fabric that has been marked with thin placement lines.

⁎ Place and sew the upright weavers first, then add the crosswise and bottom weavers.

⁎ Position the top weaver after the flower stems have been sewn.

Fig. 18. *FOLK ART ROSES, Basket of Roses and Berries block, page 32*

Gather ye rosebuds while ye may,
Old Time is still a-flying;
And this same flower that smiles today
Tomorrow will be dying.

Robert Herrick 1591–1674
"To the Virgins, to Make Much of Time"

Garden
of
Quilts

Folk Art Roses

I chose the more graphic and simple rose patterns for this quilt's collection of blocks. A limited palette of shaded fabrics for the roses and leaves helps to unify the diverse patterns. Using a variety of background fabrics in shades of tan and subtle prints gives the quilt a casual appearance. The meandering vine border with simple roses was inspired by the border of a poke stalk (or pokeweed) quilt made by Elizabeth Currier Foster as she headed west on the Oregon Trail in 1846.

FOLK ART ROSES (64" x 72"). The blocks were hand appliquéd and hand quilted by the author. The border was machine quilted by Rosalie Williams, Waikoloa, Hawaii, with assistance from Shirley Marino, Manchester, New Hampshire.

Lancaster Rose

This popular and classic pattern makes a lovely one-block quilt. Each rose could be made from the same or different colors. Each layer of the rose can be stitched as one piece of fabric or subdivided into individual petals appliquéd separately. The leaves can be enhanced with accent embroidery stitched in the veins. The center of the rose was first reverse appliquéd with a darker golden yellow, then a lighter yellow circle was appliquéd on top of the inlaid circle for a layered effect.

This pattern, circa 1865, is symbolic of early folk-art album quilts from the Pennsylvania Dutch. Hearts were often included in blocks intended for bridal quilts. The crossed stems are joined together with a circle, representing the joining of a man and a woman in marriage and their new life together as one. The full buds, just bursting to open, represent the couple's new life ahead. Although I stitched this block with just two colors of fabric, you could easily add leaves and hearts of different colors.

Folk Art Roses
in Blue Vase

This stylized rose was cut from three shades of fabrics in a simple but elegant and timeless design. Notice that, in the main flower, the center petal is a medium value. The second layer of petals is the lightest one, and the outermost petals are the darkest. This layering gives the illusion of a lush blossom. The side buds are simply flat appliquéd. Their petals can be enhanced with embroidered details, if you choose.

This classic pattern is found on many album quilts. The leaves and stems can be cut from one piece of fabric, as I have done, or the leaves can be joined separately for added contrast and a sharper stem angle. The rosebuds are enhanced with outline embroidery to divide each bud into three petals.

Rose
Chain

This pattern could be called Ring Around the Rosy. The ring chain is appliquéd as one piece of fabric, but it can also be stitched with two overlapping bias strips of the same or different colors for a woven look. The center-piece rose is padded with batting, and embroidery accents the floral details in the center of the flower and on the petals. Leaves, in two contrasting shades of green, frame and enhance the rose.

The maker of this rose quilt stitched a political statement into her quilt, circa 1860. Women had no voice in politics in the early years of our country, but their quilts could speak, without words, of their political affiliations. The petals in my Whig Rose are individually stitched in various shades of wine, ranging from dark on the outermost petals to light in the center, for a layered look (see Gradated Petals, page 15).

Basket of Roses and Berries

A simple basket of narrow fabric strips, which holds an arrangement of flowers and berries, is fun to sew (see Woven Baskets, page 22). The centerpiece rose is made from one piece of fabric, and the petals are defined with contrasting embroidery. Two different shades of floss can be twisted together for a shaded look. The berries can be embroidered, but mine are needle-turn appliquéd for a circle of fabric slightly larger than one-fourth inch. The stitching can be a challenge, but there's a feeling of satisfaction when completed.

This particular Rose of Sharon is an unusual design, created by Rena Coon Thomas of Sharon, Illinois, in 1860. The Rose of Sharon is one of the most common of the floral designs for quiltmakers of the nineteenth century. Because the design was so popular (the name was given to many rose blocks and wedding quilts), it has many variations and interpretations. I stitched a flat appliquéd sugar-cookie rose on this block and enhanced the petals and rose center with embroidery stitches in contrasting colors.

Bud Wreath

Faye Labanaris

This circle wreath of one dozen rosebuds is very simple, very sweet, as well as quick and easy to sew. The buds can be flat appliquéd, or you can use folded fabric for a subtle dimensional effect (see page 19 for folded buds). The bud cases can be made quickly and easily by cutting the shapes from Ultrasuede®. Be sure to cut on the drawn line because this material needs no turn-under allowance. Use an embroidered outline stitch to enhance the outer edges of the bud cases.

This Rose of Sharon variation, circa 1885, is most like the traditional pattern with its centerpiece rose, stems, and leaves. This block conveys the feeling of a windblown rose with its bending stems. I made the centerpiece rose with two layers of contrasting fabric. A padded under-base gives the rose some dimension, which is enhanced by an embroidered center with a lot of French knots and outline stitching.

Rose Bush

This simple bouquet design, united with a curly twist at the base, reminded me of a growing rose, hence the new name "Rose Bush" for this previously unnamed pattern. These easy sugar cookie flat roses are appliquéd and enhanced with a simple golden circle center. The bud cases, in a light shade of green, are outline stitched with dark green embroidery floss for needed contrast. Without this stitching, the bud cases could disappear into the background fabric.

The motif in the center of this pattern is reminiscent of the snowflake paper cutting done by the Pennsylvania Dutch. By stitching this motif in a shade of dark blue, I introduced another color into the block and the quilt. Simple appliquéd sugar cookie roses radiate outward from the center motif. French knots enhance the yellow center circle.

A Country Rose Garden

The block setting of this quilt was inspired by the beautiful rose gardens I have long admired on my many trips to England. I especially love the country rose gardens with their simplicity and informality. The roses just seem to grow everywhere and tumble over stone walls. The spray rose appliqués are stitched on hand-dyed, blue-sky fabric. The blocks are hand quilted with a gold metallic thread to represent golden rays of sunshine. The center medallion area of green fabrics represents the lush green lawns of the English gardens and the many shades of green in the countryside. The Rosebud Cross Spray cornerstone blocks have a quarter sun quilted in the outer corners from which the sunrays radiate downward and outward over all the roses, bathing them in sunshine. Each rose is made of different colors of fabric to represent the wonderful variety in rose coloration.

A Country Rose Garden (64" x 64"), hand appliquéd, hand pieced, and hand quilted by the author

Trumpet Rose

This 1862 pattern is a foundation rose based on a Rose of Sharon variation. The center-piece rose is composed of overlapping petals of a shaded sateen fabric. The center of the rose is detailed with embroidered stamens and French knots. The trumpet leaves radiating out from the center inspired me to name this previously unnamed block. Green fabrics with gold metallic detail add sparkle to the leaves. Embroidery lightens the look of the bud stems.

I tried to capture the beauty of a pair of simple roses I saw growing in Anne Hathaway's garden in Stratford-upon-Avon, England. This simple pink rose, called Eglantine or Sweet Brier, was a favorite of William Shakespeare and often used by him in his poems. Each flower center has a mass of single radiating strands of golden embroidery floss and French knots. In this rose, more in the center is much better than less. A thin green trim is used for the stems to give a delicate look to the rose arrangement.

Rose Tree

This pattern is adapted from a rare old quilt from Switzerland. The wholecloth roses were cut from a shaded golden yellow, hand-painted fabric. The reverse-appliquéd petal openings are outlined stitched with a contrasting single strand of golden yellow floss. The rose base is also outline stitched with the same floss. This effect, which is subtle but noticeable, adds a nice touch to the rose. The stems are bias silk cording, glue-basted into position and blindstitched in place. The base is a brown fabric to represent the earth from which the rose tree grows.

Rosebud Cross Spray
(variation 1)

This classic rosebud cross spray is stitched in a traditional manner with narrow fabric stems that have four layers of fabric for a padded look. A green printed fabric bud case and flat solid red fabric bud result in a simple, yet elegant effect.

Rose Duet

This pair of 1850 roses is stitched with golden yellow hand-painted fabric to pay tribute to the song "The Yellow Rose of Texas." The wholecloth base has a padded layer and is outline stitched with floss in a contrasting shade of yellow to add a finishing touch to the rose. The petals are appliquéd onto the wholecloth base as a unit, and then the completed rose unit is stitched to the background fabric. The rose stems are made from decorative green trim that is glue-basted and couched.

This contemporary looking stylized seg-mented rose, although designed over 140 years ago, looks ahead of its time. My hats off to the maker! A selection of fabrics with subtle shading will make the rose segments fun to stitch. Be sure to use a wide variety of greens in tones and prints for the leaves. A print green fabric for the stem completes this block.

Art Deco Rose

One Rose

This wholecloth rose, based on an 1844 block, has a padded base to give it dimension. The individual petals are stitched with three strands of embroidery floss to outline them. The center is composed of single-strand, straight stitches and masses of French knots. The leaves were individually selected from a hand-marbleized fabric with the help of a window template. The stem was cut from the same leaf fabric for an elegant look. A dark green, Ultra-suede® bud case provides a contrast in texture.

These roses, from an 1881 pattern, look like they are growing in the garden and standing up proud and beautiful. A rose-printed fabric yielded two realistic full-blown roses and a bud. Just select your rose, cut beyond the printed image, and needle-turn the edges, following the intricate petal shapes as best you can. The leaves are from a shaded, hand-painted green fabric. Arranging them from lighter green near the roses to darker green farther away creates an effect resembling sunlight shining on the roses.

Rosebud Cross Spray
(variation 2)

This cross spray of rosebuds is from an 1881 pattern. All the stems and bud cases are cut from one piece of green batik. The leaves are added separately to create sharper stem angles. Flat, pink rosebuds are inserted into the bud cases. The result is elegant and classic. You can, of course, break down the pattern and stitch the stems and bud cases as separate components. The added benefit would be that you could vary the fabric selection for each component.

This unusual rose spray design is from a very old quilt. The centerpiece, a full-blown rose, is cut as one piece from a sateen fabric with many shades of red and orange. A padded base adds some dimension to this rose. The petals and center are heavily embroidered to add richness. The rosebuds, in Ultrasuede® bud cases, are folded to add more dimension to the quilt. Batik green leaves and simple straight-stitch embroidery with two strands of floss give the illusion of a hairy rose stem. Two different colors of floss can be worked together to create a shaded look to the hairy thorns.

Moss Rose Appliqué

This pattern was an original design made by Mrs. Susan B. Stayman in 1853. In 1855, her quilt took first prize at the fair in Galesburg, Illinois. This classic beauty is brought into the twenty-first century by the use of a printed fabric for the full-blown rose. A padded base and lightly quilted petals emphasize the fabric's design. The thorns along the main stem are embroidered with two strands of floss. The innermost points and valleys of the Ultrasuede® bud case are outline embroidered with a single strand of lighter green floss for a subtle shaded effect.

The focal point for this 1849 block is the cutout design in the center. I think of it as flowerpots around a courtyard. A dark green single strand of embroidery floss outlines the center "courtyard" for a shadow effect. The roses are wholecloth with a padded layer underneath. The petals are emphasized with chain stitching, and French knots and radiating straight stitches fill the rose centers. The stems are embroidered for a delicate look to the rose grouping.

Flowerpots and Roses

Renoir's Rose Garden

A fabric medley called Renoir's Village, by Moda Fabrics, inspired the name for this quilt. Because the blocks are set on point, it requires 13 blocks to form the top. Having only 12 blocks, I added a rose courtyard print from the medley as the center-piece, with the rose blocks encircling it as they would around a garden courtyard. All the roses in this quilt are from a single piece of fabric. It is a cotton sateen, with a variety of shades ranging from yellow to red orange to dark rose.

RENOIR'S ROSE GARDEN (66" x 66"). The blocks were hand appliquéd and hand quilted by the author. The quilting patterns for the blocks were inspired by a design by Marion Newell, Eastham, Massachusetts. The sashing and borders were hand quilted by Eugenia Barnes, Marcellus, New York.

A Rose Wreath

This lovely simple wreath, circa 1850, of a half-dozen sugar cookie roses has a circular stem of decorative trim for textural interest. The roses are padded and have a lot of embroidered detail to accent the flower centers.

A classic stitching technique known as ruching creates a textured dimensional centerpiece rose for this open wreath design, circa 1852. Stem work of silk cording balances the dimension of the rose with the flatness of the leaves.

Crossed Branches Wreath

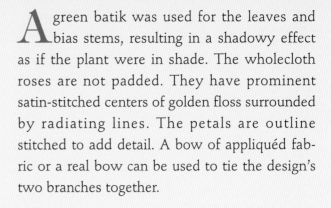

A green batik was used for the leaves and bias stems, resulting in a shadowy effect as if the plant were in shade. The wholecloth roses are not padded. They have prominent satin-stitched centers of golden floss surrounded by radiating lines. The petals are outline stitched to add detail. A bow of appliquéd fabric or a real bow can be used to tie the design's two branches together.

This bouquet block of three roses and smaller blossoms, circa 1860, lends itself to many possible color combinations. The padded wholecloth roses with embroidered accents make up the floral centerpiece of this bouquet. Smaller blossoms of Four-petal Dimensional Posies (page 16) complete the arrangement. Narrow dark green trim was glue-basted into position for a crisp, clean stem. The bouquet's bow is a piece of real ribbon tied into a bow, pressed flat, and sewn in place.

Mrs. Mann's Crossed Branches

This lovely asymmetrical design, circa 1849, of crossed branches has many variations, depending on the whim of the maker. The flowers used in this block are the Four-Petal Dimensional Posies (page 16). Silk cording adds textural interest and balance to the design's construction. The flower centers of the posies are accented with yellow French knots. These blossoms are fun to make and add a delightful look to the block.

This classic design, from about 1845, was very popular in album quilts. Satin cording makes this wreath's half-circle stem easy to construct. Padded roses, with heavily embroidered details, add complexity to the simple wholecloth roses. The leaves, cut from one piece of hand-painted fabric, have shades ranging from very light to very dark. Selecting a fabric with a lot of variation will provide you with many options for cutting leaves.

A Three Rose Wreath

A simple open wreath design, circa 1881, of three roses and a pair of buds is enhanced with embellished details. Simple sugar cookie roses are accented with an embroidered outline around the outer edge. The individual petals are emphasized with embroidery. The centers of the flowers are softened with radiating lines of embroidery and many French knots. Bud cases of Ultrasuede® hold folded rosebuds for a dimensional look.

Mrs. Kretsinger's Rose

This popular design, also known as the original Whig Rose, is often included in album quilts. It is fun to make, and sometimes, it is composed without leaves and just rosebuds encircling it. Three layers of fabric form the foundation rose. The center in my block is filled with a complex collection of knotted yarns and threads couched onto a base, with French knots and beads in many shades and textures. The center took longer to make than sewing the rose, but it was a lot of fun. This design is often used as a one-block quilt.

Mrs. Mann's Wreath Spray

This design, circa 1849, features a drooping branch of roses in various stages of bloom, ranging from tight buds to full-blown flowers. Decorative brown picot edge trim adds interest and makes it easy to form the design's stems. Using window templates on just one piece of fabric, I was able to have color control over the selection of petal components for the three upright blooms. The full-blown rose is embroidered with many varying shades of rose to yellow orange. A fabric circle forms the simple center of the flower, with no embroidered accents.

An olive green batik with dark green accents was used for the bias stem and leaves of this wreath. The three-pronged bud cases were cut from Ultrasuede®. Each case is stitched down along the outer edge, forming a pocket to receive the folded fabric rosebud. The prongs are also stitched to the top layer of the rosebuds. A tiny bit of batting was added before the final stitches were taken for a padded bud.

Birds and Blossoms Wreath

The addition of a pair of blue birds adds interest and a romantic touch to this crossed branch wreath, circa 1850, often found on bridal quilts. A pair of roses symbolizes the bride and groom, and the two tiny flowers represent the new life to come. Each of the two tiny blossoms is made by gathering a circle of fabric, much like making a yo-yo (see Four-Petal Dimensional Posies, page 16).

This block was inspired by an 1840s wreath with chintz roses on a chintz-work quilt. The stem is constructed in two colors of narrow trim, green and brown. The trim is glue-basted into position before being stitched securely in place. The wholecloth roses are padded and embroidered to separate the petals and to create the center details. A variety of shaded green leaves completes the wreath.

Intertwined Wreath

Faye Labanaris ✳ **Appliqué Rose Garden**

Fancy Roses

For the last dozen blocks in this series, which includes rose arrangements in vases and baskets, I chose to set the blocks in a formal setting reminiscent of the fancy Baltimore Album quilts that contain the ultimate in elaborate album blocks. I used a polished ecru cotton fabric and beautiful hand-painted fabrics for roses of many colors. The border is set off from the blocks by a sashing strip made up of all the blue fabrics used in the vases and baskets. The quilt is beautifully machine quilted by Ellen Peters, Laconia, New Hampshire, in a delicate doily design, inspired from a seventeenth-century wholecloth Durham (England) quilt, and centered on each of the block intersections. Background diagonal linear quilting completes the lovely quilting design.

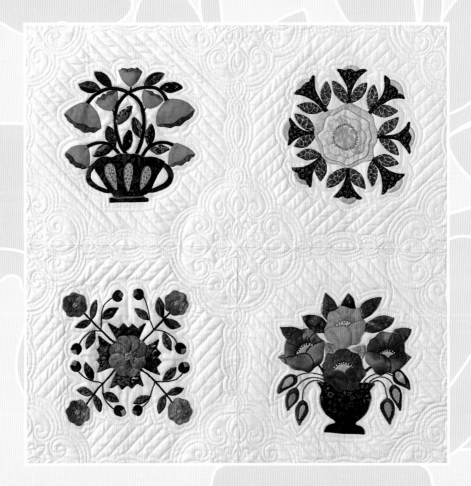

FANCY ROSES (51" x 62"). The blocks and original-design border was hand stitched by the author. Machine quilted by Ellen Peters, Laconia, New Hampshire.

Wild Rose

Faye Labanaris

This foundation rose, from a mid-1800s design, is centered on a leafy green fabric, but it could also be stitched on a rose-colored fabric for more layers. Delicate chain-stitched stems radiate out from the center rose. A variety of green prints were used to add interest to the leaves. The bud cases are fabric and are just bursting with full buds. A lovely hand-painted rose fabric resulted in many different shades of roses streaked with white to be used for lots of petal interest.

Although the block was designed in the mid-1800s, the flower has an art deco look to me. In any case, the roses are quite unlike the traditional style of roses for the era. A pair of stylized-segmented roses is the focal point of this arrangement. The simplicity of the vase is accented with gold chain-stitched embroidery. Dark green leaves and bias stems give weight to the upright roses and the buds, which are in two different stages of opening.

Rose of Sharon
(variation 2)

This Rose of Sharon variation, often called the Democrat Rose, was used in quilts to make a political statement. The roses used in this block are simple wholecloth roses with accented centers of satin stitches and French knots. The roses are outlined stitched with contrasting embroidery floss, and the stems are embroidered with a chain stitch for a delicate look. The buds are emphasized with green embroidery to delineate the individual petals. This block is often used as a lovely one-block bed quilt.

This design was inspired by an old pattern from the A. J. Anderson family of Lawrence, Kansas, in the mid-1800s. The roses are composed of two layers with two different shades of fabric. The inner layer is a dark red print, and the outer layer is a lighter solid shade of red. The individual petals can be stitched separately or embroidered, but I left the rose as one piece for simplicity. Their drooping habit reminds me of roses just past their prime. The vase has teardrop reverse appliquéd inserts of a gold calico. The openings are outlined with gold embroidery, and the rim and handles are accent embroidered for a nice finishing touch.

Conventional Rose
(Indiana)

The block design is from about 1840. The centerpiece foundation rose is composed of layered hand-painted yellow fabric. Each layer is set off with an outline stitch of a contrasting color. The innermost layer is composed of individual petals, which overlap to form a swirl of rose petals around the orange fabric center. A simple circle of thick French knots highlights this rose center.

The petals in this block, circa the mid-1800s, are appliquéd individually. A window template will allow you to select just the right colors for the petals. The petals are overlapped as they are appliquéd. The flower centers are accented with a few French knots. You could easily add more French knots and radiating stamen lines, if you like. Bias stems of a medium green print add some interest to the rose arrangement. The basket has dark blue weavers stitched on a base of a gold calico print. The handles are heavily satin stitched with contrasting dark blue outline stitching.

Rose of Sharon
(variation 3)

The centerpiece rose of this block, from a design circa 1860, is composed of individual overlapping stitched petals with a cluster of French knots in the center. The four cornerstone roses are flat open pieces with an outline stitch of a light color accenting the outer edges. The tiny circular buds have bud cases cut from Ultrasuede® for easy sewing. The stems are chain stitched with dark green embroidery floss to give the sewn design a light and airy feel.

This lush bouquet of wholecloth roses is cut from four different shades of fabric, ranging from deep wine to medium rose. The roses are heavily padded, and their centers are accented with gold satin stitching and a halo of French knots. The petals are delineated with two strands of floss and an outline stitch. The buds are reverse appliquéd on a large square of pink fabric then trimmed to size. Alternatively, you can draw the bud outline on a large square of green fabric, cut out the oval opening, stitch the opening on the pink fabric, then trim both fabrics to size.

Ohio Rose

Faye Labanaris

Pioneers in the 1850s paid tribute to their new homes by naming block designs for the state where they had settled. These blocks were often sent back to family and friends to become a part of album quilts. This rose is quite stylized with sharp petal points. It has two layers, with a center opening stitched as reverse appliqué. The center portion can be enhanced with clusters of French knots. The stems are chain stitched for a delicate look. The folded rosebuds are stitched on top of a green back layer, with the top of the bud case stitched in place to enclose the bud.

This block, from about the mid-1800s, pays tribute to the hardy old rose known as Harrison's Yellow. This rose was carried by many pioneers from their eastern homes to their new homes out west. Cuttings were left growing all along the Oregon Trail and are still found there today. Wholecloth roses with a padded layer are used in this block. The outer, segmented petals are defined by outline embroidery in a contrasting color. The rosebuds are folded to add dimension to balance out the padded roses. Split leaves surround the centerpiece rose and add more green fabrics to the block.

Virginia Rose

This rose is known as the Virginia Rose, from an original design by Caroline Stalnaker of West Virginia, circa 1855. It is a stemmed rose composition with a centerpiece rose base of individual petals. It could, of course, be stitched as a wholecloth base. The second layer of a lighter color is accented with a complex raised center of satin stitches and radiating delicate embroidered stamens with a lot of tiny French knots. The petals are emphasized with embroidery in a dark contrasting shade of wine. The leaves were selected from a fabric with printed leaves so that each leaf has a center vein.

The design for this block is from the mid-1800s. Adding a vase to a block provides an opportunity to use additional colors and prints. A beautiful shaded Baltimore blue in a delicate print works nicely for the vase. The roses are composed of two layers, one lighter and one darker. The petals on the back layer are embroidered with satin stitching, and French knots are used for the center detailing. The vase's rim is outlined with gold embroidery floss for a gilded look.

Fancy Roses Border

Enhance your quilt top with a border of scrolling vines and clusters of rose bouquets. The delicate nature of the vines, with a variety of leaves, rose buds, and dancing bellflowers, will tie the blocks together with an airy feeling of summertime's floral abundance. (The Fancy Roses Border pattern starts on page 81.)

Stems

Cut ¾" to 1" wide bias strips to make ¼" wide bias stems. Choose your favorite method of stem construction from the techniques described on pages 12–14.

Roses, buds, and bellflowers

Select the colors used throughout the rose blocks in the quilt top and mix for a random look.

Leaves

Select a number of green fabric scraps.

Embroidery details

Use floss to enhance the centers of the roses and delineate the rose petals.

BORDER CONSTRUCTION

✳ Measure the length of your quilt and cut two inner border strips 1" wide and ½" longer than the quilt measurement. Sew these strips to the sides of your quilt.

✳ Measure the width of the quilt, including the two side border strips, and cut two more inner border strips this length plus ½". Sew these to the top and bottom of your quilt.

✳ For the outer border, measure your quilt as before. Cut border strips 10" wide and add a couple of extra inches to the length.

✳ Fold each border strip in half through its length and again across the width to find its center. Use the folds as guidelines for placing the pattern. Trace the pattern on the border strips. (See the placement guide on page 83.)

✳ Appliqué the bias vines first, then add the leaves and rose bouquets to each border strip. Exact placement of the various pieces is not necessary. Finish by adding embroidery details to enhance the roses. You can add more leaves and flowers, if you like.

✳ Trim the borders to 7" to 8½" wide and trim the length to your quilt's measurements. Sew the side borders on first, then add the top and bottom borders as before.

Enjoy finishing your quilt with this colorful yet delicate border.

Fancy Roses Border

Pattern fits 7" to 8½" wide borders

Section 1

reverse
vine
here

start reverse
vine here

Fancy Roses Border

Section 2

Section 3

Section 2

Section 1

placement guide

Section 3

A Rose Garden Challenge

While I was stitching blocks for the first quilt in this series, I wondered what blocks other quilters might select and how they would set and border them. So, I issued a Rose Garden Challenge to a dozen of my friends who are also very talented quilters. The rules were simple: choose a dozen patterns from the vintage rose patterns and set the blocks and border the quilt in a pleasing and creative manner. The results are rose garden quilts from the United States and England that range from sweet simplicity to luxurious lushness. I hope you find them inspirational for your own rose garden quilt.

MÉLANGE DU ROSES *(43" x 43"), by Gail Mitchell, Bridgton, Maine. Gail chose just five rose designs for her challenge quilt. She used Virginia Rose block in a four-block center for the medallion, with four more rose blocks in the corners. The blocks are set off by a lovely floral garland border fabric. Her piece is a technique sampler because she used a different construction technique for each block of roses. The techniques include sculptured roses, ruched roses,* broderie perse, *and stuffed roses. She says she truly enjoyed the project because it was a lot of fun to try many different techniques.*

SYDNEY'S ROSE GARDEN *(53" x 44"), by Malerie Albertson, Wichita, Kansas. Malerie tells this story about the naming of her quilt: "The inspiration for my border came from gardening in my backyard with my cats. During a recent major landscaping project, when tired, I sat on the patio and watched the birds on the feeder. (Neither of the cats was able to catch the birds, to their dismay.) In the early morning, we had goldfinches and cardinals. When I dug in the garden, a robin would hop about three feet from me as I threw worms to him, and of course, the little sparrows were everywhere, teasing my cats. When I planted some rose bushes, the cats liked to rest under them and hide in the cool dirt.*

"When I started to make this quilt, Sydney was just a kitten learning about the outdoors. It was so much fun to watch her learning to catch bugs and leaves with her sister, Babie, by her side. That is why I named the quilt SYDNEY'S ROSE GARDEN."

MASQUERADE *(52" x 49"), by Lorna M. Hunter, Ponteland, Northumberland, England. Lorna is a gifted gardener and flower arranger as well as a quilter. In her description of her challenge quilt, she writes, "Peeping in at the window, as I sit sewing, is a lovely rose called Masquerade. It fascinates me because the flowers change color from bright yellow to pink and dark red. In a gardening magazine, it was described as 'a trifle overpowering for anyone with a nervous disposition.'*

"Having been an enthusiastic flower arranger, I suppose it was inevitable that my placement of the rose blocks should resemble a flower arrangement, with the flower colors chosen by following a series of imaginary triangles. I have enjoyed working on this piece and have embellished the flower centers with beads and French knots worked in silk ribbon and silk thread."

WOODLAND ROSES *(32" x 50"), by Mercy Arrastia, Miami, Florida. Although Mercy's Rose Garden quilt has fewer than a dozen roses, it is filled with interest, beautiful roses, and hand-dyed fabrics. The alternate background blocks progress from green to brown to give the quilt a "lost in the woods" feeling. Mercy collected beautiful dyed and reproduction fabrics in all her travels, and her garden quilt reflects the richness of her collection. Gold metallic radiating spirals are quilted in the background of each rose block.*

Mercy's favorite appliqué method is marking the background fabric on the back, placing the appliqué fabric on the front of the background, and hand basting along the line on the back. She then turns the piece over, and trims the appliqué piece to a scant ¼" from the basted line. She cuts every other basting stitch, pulls out a strand and needle-turn appliqués, following the perforated basting line visible on the appliqué and background fabric.

DAD'S ANNIVERSARY ROSE GARDEN (64" x 64"), by Elizabeth Devlin, East Falmouth, Massachusetts. "My father gave my mother a rose bush each year on their anniversary," Elizabeth remembers. "He was an avid vegetable gardener, but Mom took care of the flower garden. Although some of the roses have died over the years, a great many are still in bloom."

Liz stitched this quilt as tribute to her dad. Although she chose nine blocks set three by three, her blocks are far from traditional. She selected three different sizes for her blocks: 9", 12", and 15". They are framed by vibrant pink floral fabric and sashed with many shades of garden green fabrics. This quilt makes one smile with its bright and cheery appearance.

A DOZEN RED ROSES FOR MOM

(AKA THE WAR OF THE ROSES) (44" x 44"), by Marylou McDonald, Laurel, Maryland. Marylou explains her title, "The quilt is titled for the dozen roses my dad gave my mother each month for the first year that they were married. He continued to give her a dozen red roses on their anniversary each year thereafter. The quilt was also named WAR OF THE ROSES because I began this quilt on March 20, 2003, the day that the war with Iraq started."

Marylou reduced the 7" design area of the patterns by 71 percent to create a 5" block design. The center medallion, which is 10" x 10", includes all the prominent flowers from the other 12 blocks in the quilt. The border, 7" x 44", is a vine with all the flowers from the blocks. The trapunto quilting contains the drooping rose design around the center block and between the blocks and border.

A ROSE BY ANY OTHER NAME

(68" x 68"), by Jo Ann Joy, Silverhill, Alabama. Jo Ann enlarged the blocks 143 percent for a 10" design area. Her medallion setting of 12 blocks includes a four-block center of rose sprays, followed by a round of flowers in baskets and vases. The outermost triangular corners are set with wreath blocks. Beautiful quilting separates the large, on-point center from the triangular corners.

A YEAR OF VINES AND ROSES *(48" x 50"), by Nancy Jones Hansen, Center Sandwich, New Hampshire. The blocks are set in an asymmetrical manner to balance with the meandering, asymmetrical border. The border is based on a painting technique called "stamping." Nancy cuts her own stamps to match her fabrics and décor. "Stamping is really the opposite of stenciling," Nancy says. "A stamp in the desired shape is cut out of a porous, flexible rubber material. Leaves and petals can have vines cut into them, or other details. I put fabric paint on the stamp and stamp it on the fabric.*

"The vines are arranged freehand and filled in with leaves and flowers. Roses and other flowers are quilted into the border to fill in the empty spaces. This is not an original technique, but rather one that I saw more than 10 years ago in a home decorating magazine. The fun part is that, if someplace is sparse, I can always add another vine to fill it in. It is very forgiving."

NANA'S ROSES *(41" x 41")*, *by Deborah Fournier-Johnstone, Dover, New Hampshire. Deborah recalls,* "My inspiration for this wallhanging comes from my memories of my Nana's rose garden in Paisley, Scotland. I have fond memories of one particular visit during the summer of 1968. Nana's roses were in full bloom and very pink. I spent day after day plucking rose petals from the blooms to make rose perfume. Nana never complained about my picking her roses apart, and she graciously wore my perfume with pleasure. Nana has since passed away, but her roses are still blooming and enjoyed by all who pass by her 'wee house' on Ladykirk Crescent."

Deborah stitched this delicate four-block wallhanging as a loving tribute to her Nana. Her choice of fabrics and embroidered border trim make a perfect combination for the designs she chose to stitch.

FLORAL FANTASY *(50" x 40")*, *by Stephanie Halliwell, Mount Sinai, New York. Stephanie (nicknamed Steve) wanted her quilt to be different, so she used black fabric for strong contrast. She used the Ring of Roses block, along with a variety of six different spray rose patterns for a classic three-by-four block set. The blocks are heavily embellished with a lot of beads, ribbons, and different threads. The result is truly a fantasy garden of delightful flowers that are fun to admire.*

The border is quilted with variegated thread in an old quilting design from Northumberland, England. The wholecloth Durham quilts of the area are noted for their beautiful quilting motifs. Steve chose a small fern design to enhance her border and tie the quilt to her English roots. The binding of the quilt is composed of variegated fabrics to tie in all the different colors of roses.

FOREST ROSES (48" x 48"), by Geriann Athans, Plymouth, New Hampshire. Geriann says, "The design for this quilt came from a desire to use some of my landscape sketches rather than using a traditional block setting. The two ideas literally merged just before I fell asleep one night, and stayed with me for a long time. Once I sat down to sew, every piece simply fell into place. The roses are made with just about every technique and material, including silk, Ultrasuede®, and broderie perse, with embroidery added in. It was fun to landscape my scene with the various rose patterns."

WATER GARDEN (36" x 52"), by Barbara Marion Hartshorn, Leicester, England. Barbara chose seven patterns for her unique interpretation of the challenge. The inspiration for the block setting came from an English tile in the Early Twentieth Century Tile Collection, at the Taggart Museum in Great Staughton, Huntingdon, United Kingdom. Because embroidery is her first love and quilting her second, she combined the two for a stunning and unique result.

Each block is a different size. They are framed with a golden metallic fabric in a Moorish window-type opening, accented with a lot of embroidery. Each of the blocks has complex embroidered details done in an old embroidery technique known as stump work. The result is three-dimensional flowers, leaves, and insects with extraordinary detail that you can't stop admiring.

Acknowledgments

This book is the result of many people working together to produce this final product. I would like to thank, with heartfelt gratitude, the following people for helping me:

To the American Quilter's Society and publisher Meredith Schroeder for giving me the opportunity to produce a fourth book with them. I appreciate all the support and enthusiasm that I have received from AQS since publishing my first book, Blossoms by the Sea.

To my editor, Barbara Smith, for being there with me ever since I wrote my second book with AQS, Quilts with a View. Your gift of a gentle attitude and understanding ear makes your skillful editing of the manuscript painless for me to accept any of the cuts and changes. Your encouragement and excitement with this, our third book together, are most gratifying.

To Eugenia Barnes, thank you for listening with your heart and being there from the conception of this project to its completion. Your insight and understanding of the work of our album ancestors and your encouragement of my attempt to bring their patterns into the twenty-first century helped me more than I can say. Thank you for taking RENOIR'S ROSE GARDEN as a top and basting it, then quilting the sashing and borders when time was a factor for me. I value your tiny stitches on the quilt.

To Ellen Peters for helping me, throughout the process of creating the quilts and writing books, with a listening ear and expert advice. Thank you for working your magic talents again with your beautiful machine quilting on FANCY ROSES.

To JoAnn Joy and Brenda Perguson for coming to my aid to beautifully sandwich and baste FOLK ART ROSES.

To Marylou MacDonald for sending me a lovely assortment of fabrics to use for the vases in FANCY ROSES.

For my sister, Joanna Samaras, and for Shirley Marino, thank you for cutting all the blocks for FANCY ROSES.

To the 12 quilters who enthusiastically participated in being a part of the Dozen Roses/Rose Garden challenge. Your excitement at seeing the 48 patterns was encouraging to me during the early stages of book writing. Thank you for creating unique Rose Garden quilts and for allowing your quilts to be included in this book and sharing them with the world.

To my husband, Nick, for going above and beyond the call of duty during the "for better or worse phase" of this book. I couldn't have made it without you. Thank you for your love, your care, and continual support.

And last but not least, to the quiltmakers of long ago who so loved roses and wanted to stitch them on cloth. Your loving legacy is still with us today and is preserved in this volume for our children and grandchildren to enjoy.

Bibliography

Bowman, Doris M. *The Smithsonian Treasury of American Quilts.*
Washington, D.C.: Smithsonian Institution Press, 1991.

Brackman, Barbara. *Encyclopedia of Applique.*
McLean, VA: EPM Publications, Inc., 1994.

Bullard, Lacy Folmar and Shiell, Betty Jo. *Chintz Quilts: Unfading Glory.*
Tallahassee, FL: Serendipity Publishers, 1983.

Cross, Mary Bywater. *Treasures in the Trunk.*
Nashville, TN: Rutledge Hill Press, 1993.

Finley, Ruth E. *Old Patchwork Quilts and the Women Who Made Them.*
McLean, VA: EPM Publications, 1992.

Goldsborough, Jennifer Faulds. *Lavish Legacies.*
Laurel MD: S&S Graphics, 1994.

Havig, Bettina. *Carrie Hall Blocks.*
Paducah, KY: American Quilter's Society, 1999.

Katzenberg, Dena S. *Baltimore Album Quilts.*
Baltimore, MD: The Baltimore Museum of Art, 1980.

Khin, Yvonne M. *The Collector's Dictionary of Quilt Names & Patterns.*
Washington, D.C.: Acropolis Books, LTD, 1980.

Kimball, Jeana. *Red and Green: An Appliqué Tradition.*
Bothell, WA: That Patchwork Place, 1990.

Kolter, Jane Bentley. *Forget Me Not.*
New York: Sterling Publishing Company, 1985.

Sienkiewicz, Elly. *Baltimore Beauties and Beyond, Vol. I.*
Lafayette, California: C&T Publishing, 1989.

Sienkiewicz, Elly. *Baltimore Beauties and Beyond, Vol. II.*
Lafayette, California: C&T Publishing, 1991.

Sienkiewicz, Elly. *The Best of Baltimore Beauties.*
Lafayette, California: C&T Publishing, 2000.

Resources

EUGENIA BARNES
2524 Platt Road
Marcellus, NY 13108
E-mail: Muzzy37@aol.com
AQS-certified appraiser;
workshops, lectures, and classes

FLOWER GARDEN RIBBONS
80 Mt. Vernon Street
Dover, NH 03820
E-mail: fayequilt@comcast.net
Ribbons and trims

FAYE LABANARIS
80 Mt. Vernon Street
Dover, NH 03820
Workshops, lectures, and classes

MICKEY LAWLER
Skydyes
PO Box 370116
West Hartford, CT 06137
www.skydyes.com
*Handpainted cottons and silks;
workshops, lectures, and classes*

ELLEN PETERS
27 Tremont Street
Laconia, NH 03246
E-mail: ebpeters@Lr.net
Custom machine quilting;
Workshops, lectures, and classes

Index

About the Author

Faye Labanaris specializes in hand appliqué, including Baltimore Album and Hawaiian, as well as ribbon-work appliqué with dimensional flowers made with French wire-edge ribbon and silk. Formerly a high school biology teacher and science consultant for the city of Dover, New Hampshire, elementary schools, Faye enjoys teaching and eagerly shares her knowledge with her students. She offers classes to all levels of quilters, inspiring beginners as well as challenging advanced quilters. She has taught in Hawaii, throughout the continental United States, and throughout Great Britain.

In 1994, the author was voted National Honored Teacher by her students nationwide in C&T's and Elly Sienkiewicz's first Baltimore Album Revival Contest. Her quilt A TRIBUTE TO CELIA THAXTER placed first in its category, Reflective of a Particular Life and Time. That quilt became the basis for her first book, *Blossoms by the Sea*. Her quilt AN ENGLISH COTTAGE GARDEN placed third in the Innovative category in the second Baltimore Revival contest. This quilt inspired Faye to write *Garden View Appliqué*. She has twice been a winner in the Great American Quilt Festival sponsored by the Museum of American Folk Art, and her work has been included in several of Elly Sienkiewicz's *Baltimore Beauties and Beyond* series.

Faye is the co-producer and founder of Quilt Hawaii, a quilt show and conference held each year, in early July, on a different Hawaiian island. She also co-produces Quilt Ventures' Tours for Quilters, with trips to England, Lancaster County, Philadelphia, New England in autumn, and Paducah in the spring for the AQS show. Her husband and two sons have been very supportive of her endeavors.

She has written three books: *Blossoms by the Sea: Making Ribbon Flowers for Quilts* (out of print), *Quilts with a View: A Fabric Adventure,* and *Garden View Applique: Vintage Album Patterns,* all published by the American Quilter's Society.

Visit www.quiltventures.com for information about Quilt Hawaii and Quilt Ventures Tours.

Other AQS Books

This is only a small selection of the books available from the American Quilter's Society. AQS books are known worldwide for timely topics, clear writing, beautiful color photos, and accurate illustrations and patterns. The following books are available from your local bookseller, quilt shop, or public library.

#6800   us$22.95

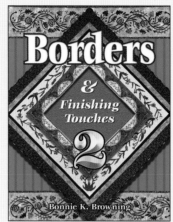

#6804   us$22.95

#6072   us$25.95

#6211   us$19.95

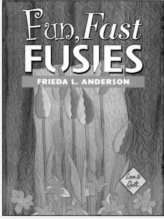

#6801   us$19.95

#6674   us$19.95

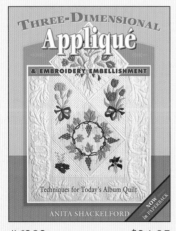

#6292   us$24.95

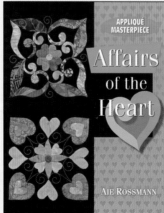

#6517   us$21.95

#6511   us$22.95

Look for these books nationally.
Call or **Visit** our Web site at

1-800-626-5420
www.AmericanQuilter.com